The Top
10
Distinctions Between Entrepreneurs and Employees

KEITH CAMERON SMITH

BALLANTINE BOOKS

NEW YORK

The Top
10
Distinctions Between
Entrepreneurs and
Employees

Published in the United States by Ballantine Books,
an imprint of The Random House Publishing Group,
a division of Random House, Inc., New York.

BALLANTINE and colophon are registered trademarks
of Random House, Inc.

Library of Congress Cataloging-in-Publication Data
Smith, Keith Cameron.
The top 10 distinctions between entrepreneurs and employees /
Keith Cameron Smith.
p.   cm.
ISBN 978-0-345-53550-4 (hardcover : alk. paper)
eBook ISBN 978-0-345-53551-1
1. Entrepreneurship.   2. Employees.   3. Success in
business.   I. Title.   II Title: Top ten distinctions between
entrepreneurs and employees.
HB615.S65 2012
658.4'21—dc23
2012021299

Printed in the United States of America on acid-free paper

www.ballantinebooks.com

2 4 6 8 9 7 5 3 1

First Edition

Title-page photographs: © Masterfile Royalty Free (people),
© Photodisc (light bulb)

Book design by Victoria Wong

Foreword

BY SHARON LECHTER

When it comes to money, I have found that the most important difference between the rich and the poor is found in their mindsets. In fact, I would say that your mindset may be more important than your bank account as a measure of your financial future. A rich person with a poor mindset will most likely lose his or her wealth. In contrast, many people who are wealthy today started out very poor, with nothing in material wealth, but they had the desire to become rich and trained themselves to have a rich mindset. With a rich mindset, they know that even if they have financial setbacks they can and will regain their wealth. They understand the importance of entrepreneurship.

You are holding a book that can give you a considerable advantage in your journey to becoming a successful entrepreneur. The ideas that Keith presents here are powerful and practical. He shares some fresh insights and perspectives from his own life experiences that are congruent with the messages that I have been teaching throughout my life.

It was Napoleon Hill, author of *Think and Grow Rich,* who said, "Whatever the mind can conceive and believe, it can achieve. Man, alone, has the power to transform his thoughts into physical reality; man, alone, can dream and make his dreams come true." But Hill also knew that this power of the mind is strengthened best by learning from adversity and overcoming fear. I have had the honor to work with the Napoleon Hill Foundation in my latest books, *Three Feet from Gold* and *Outwitting the Devil,* both of

which share how to discover your own Personal
Success Equation, turn your fear into faith, and
achieve the success you deserve.

In this book, Keith highlights and specifically
addresses the differences in mindset that allow
an entrepreneur to create success, both financially and personally. Whether you are an aspiring entrepreneur or already have a thriving
business, these distinctions will help you create
success and fulfillment on your journey. If you
are an employee, these distinctions can help you
to think and act more like an entrepreneur and
become more valuable to your company. You
will also benefit from Keith's distinctions on
powerful ways to work with people. Successful
entrepreneurs understand that all business is
about people and learning how to relate and
communicate well with people is a very necessary skill to develop.

These distinctions may offer you an advantage in your professional life, and may also

reveal great ideas on how to improve your personal life. A true entrepreneur adds value to the world and in doing so creates a successful business. Along the way this same entrepreneur will find equal or greater rewards in his or her personal life. The distinctions in this book will empower you to improve every area of your life.

Keith has a gift in being able to connect and communicate with people in ways that inspire them to believe in themselves and encourage them to take action. As you read this book you will experience that gift. We hope it will give you a clearer vision for your own life and a better understanding of how to achieve the success and freedom you deserve.

May you be blessed with success,
Sharon Lechter

Along with being a bestselling author, SHARON LECHTER is a CPA, entrepreneur, international speaker, and proud mother and grandmother. She is also a national spokesperson for the AICPA for financial literacy and was a member of the first President's Advisory Council on Financial Literacy and founder of Pay Your Family First. Her latest books released in cooperation with the Napoleon Hill Foundation include *Three Feet from Gold* and *Outwitting the Devil.* Also available is her award-winning, money-and-life reality-based board game, "ThriveTime for Teens." She is also the co-author of the international bestselling book *Rich Dad, Poor Dad.*

Preface

Since writing *The Top 10 Distinctions Between Millionaires and the Middle Class,* I have continued to learn some valuable lessons about business and life. So I wrote this book because I wanted to share some of the fresh insights and perspectives I have gained over the last few years. This book reveals more personal stories of my successes and failures that have not been in my previous books.

I have been an entrepreneur for the last two decades and have experienced some great successes. I have also had some experiences that seemed like terrible failures at the time, but the lessons I learned from these failures transformed them into successes, and led me to more success. The lessons you can learn from your own failures are extremely valuable. As long as you are willing to embrace your experiences by taking full responsibility for them, your mistakes and failures will become some of the most powerfully enlightening experiences of your life.

The knowledge you have gained from your own past is the power you need to create your future. However, you will not learn from your past failures if you blame others for or complain about them, or try to justify why you didn't succeed. In order to become a successful entrepreneur you must keep moving forward toward the future you desire. Blaming, complaining, and attempting to justify keep you stuck in the past. One of the distinctions in this book includes a personal story of the largest business failure I have ever experienced and the important lessons I learned from it. I share it because I believe that if you want to impress someone you tell them of your successes, but if you want to impact someone you tell them of your failures. I wrote this book because I want to impact you.

There are three other reasons why I wrote this book and am now developing this series: responsibility, purpose, and legacy. I believe we all have a responsibility to share those things that produce positive results in our lives. I experience a strong sense of purpose each time I teach these distinctions at various venues around the world. And I see these books as part of my legacy, especially to my own children. Some of my favorite books are more than one hundred years old. It's fascinating to think that someone may be reading, enjoying, and benefiting from this book a hundred years from now. I strongly believe that these distinctions between entrepreneurs and employees are timeless. They are just as relevant today as they were one hundred years ago and will be just as relevant one hundred years from now. Read, enjoy, and benefit from these distinctions. You can become a successful entrepreneur.

Contents

CONTENTS

The Top
10
Distinctions Between Entrepreneurs and Employees

Entrepreneurs educate themselves more than they entertain themselves.

Employees entertain themselves more than they educate themselves.

The best education entrepreneurs can receive comes from experience. Experience is the schooling for successful entrepreneurs. It provides a curriculum unlike anything the traditional school system can even begin to comprehend. Experience teaches people how to continually educate themselves, how to have an empowering perspective of failure, how to find solutions, how to know a little about a lot, how to praise and correct others, how to say "the buck stops here," how to build wealth, how to look into the future, and how to take risks because of faith.

The teachers in the school of experience want to see their students succeed, so they offer no shortcuts. Some of the teachers in the school of experience are called Failure, Rejection, Loss, Attitude, Mind-set, Forgiveness, Perseverance, Poverty, Prosperity. Experience will not allow students to drop a course just because it gets difficult. If a student does quit a class before it's finished, that student must go back to the class and pass the test before they can attend the graduation ceremony called Success. Each of the Distinctions in this little book is one of the most important lessons that the school of experience teaches entrepreneurs.

The traditional school system in the corporate world teaches people to be employees, not entrepreneurs. The traditional school system is called The Status Quo. It trains and conditions people to think about money and success from a very limited perspective. It does this by telling them what they have to learn and requiring that they obey the rules without question. In the school of experience, entrepreneurs choose what they want to learn about and they can ask any question they choose to without fear of being reprimanded or disciplined. Successful entrepreneurs ask themselves what they would really like to do with their lives, and then they ask others the questions that give them the answers to how to be successful at their chosen field of interest. The traditional school system does not teach people to think about being a successful entrepreneur. Sure, elementary school teachers may ask kids what they want to be when they grow up but the answers are related to being an employee, because that's what they are taught. Most kids say they want to be a police officer, firefighter, pilot, teacher, doctor, veterinarian, athlete. And most of the answers they give are usually, not always, geared toward being an employee. These kids are also told they must go to college if they want to get a good job.

A good job means being a good employee. There's nothing wrong with being a good employee if that's what you want to do; but there is also the option of becoming a successful entrepreneur. You cannot learn how to become a successful entrepreneur from the traditional school system.

Something strange happens to kids from their first few years of traditional school to their last few years. In the beginning they have some idea of what they want to be, but near the end of high school, they no longer know.

Ask most high school students why they're going to attend college and most of them give you a blank stare. Why do so many young men and women in the traditional school system have an idea of what they want to be when they are young, but they don't know ten years later? I believe the answer is that they have been conditioned to follow orders. After years of being told what to do, they're asked what they'd like to do and they just don't know. And you can't blame them. Since many of them are not clear on what they want to do, they go to college. They invest years of their time and a lot of money then end up not using their college education and end up in a field that has nothing to do with their schooling. Some may even say they have wasted a lot of time and money by going to college. I did not go to college. Well, I did go, for two weeks, but then dropped out and went to work as a manager at a local men's clothing store, because I believed I could learn more about business by working in one rather than hearing about one in school. I was right; the lessons I learned from experience were powerful and lasting. In the traditional school system we're given a very limited perspective of life. We're told that this is the way the world works, from people who may or may not have been pursuing their own purpose and passion. I'm not here to attack the traditional school system—I went to the traditional school system from kindergarten up through twelfth grade, and graduated. I had some remarkable teachers growing up who joined the profession because they had a passion for teaching, and truly loved kids—but in hindsight, it's obvious that many teachers were there just doing the job to get a paycheck. For me, there's not much worse than doing a job just for the money. We all have a deep need to engage in meaningful work. If your work is devoid of meaning, there's a good chance that your life will follow suit. Your work is an important part of your life, and as a result your quality of life is directly related to the choices you make about the work you engage in. As the saying goes: If you're going to climb the corporate ladder, make sure it's leaning against the right wall. In other words, if you don't enjoy your work, change your work.

Most people spend their entire lives being told what to do. It starts with their parents, continues with their teachers, and for many people, it carries on through their lives with their bosses. The great irony is that many people don't like to be told what to do. The problem is that most need to be because they have been completely conditioned to do only what other people tell them to.

The good news is that regardless of your traditional schooling and mental conditioning, you can recondition your mind. Start reconditioning your mind by educating yourself in an area you truly enjoy. Studying subjects that inspire you is a key to being successful and fulfilled.

> Start reconditioning your mind by educating yourself in an area you truly enjoy. Studying subjects that inspire you is a key to being successful and fulfilled.

My life started to change for the better the

day I realized that my education was my responsibility. Early in life others told me what I had to learn, but now I choose what I invest my time learning about. If we allow others to choose for us, and their choices are not in alignment with our heart's desires, then we feel a lack of purpose and meaning in our lives.

If you went to the traditional school system, you were taught to close your book when it was time to take a test. It's a strange approach, considering that in the real world of experience, life is an open-book exam. You can find all the answers you need to succeed simply by continuing to educate yourself. Success is not just about what and who you know, it's also about what you are choosing to learn. And that will lead to who you need to know and the opportunities that you find. Make sure you educate yourself more than you entertain yourself. Learn about yourself and then about the interest of the people you are working with or want to work with.

Limit your entertainment. Most of the entertainment in our world is foolishness. While some can be fun and a momentary release from the pressures of life, much of the entertainment people watch and listen to can cause some of the stress they are experiencing. Whatever you are consistently putting into your mind is conditioning you for the future you will live.

The meaning of *entertainment* is "to detain from entering," and most entertainment does just that: It prevents you from entering and engaging with life. When seeking to be entertained, find positive entertainment that inspires. Watch movies based on true stories that motivate you to take action. How much more action could you start taking toward your dreams if you entertained yourself less and educated yourself more? Are your dreams worth it? Of course they are. How much could you learn in the next twelve months if you turned your TV time into education time? How much would that new knowledge help you improve your standard of living and quality of life? Remember, your education is *your* responsibility.

It amazes me that most people haven't even considered what they would really love to do with their life. The reason I choose to write books and teach workshops is to help people find, focus on, and succeed at work they love to do. Finding that focus requires knowing yourself. What are your likes and dislikes? Your strengths and weaknesses? What are your personality traits? What do you love to do?

If you haven't taken a personality profile before, do it soon—it's an enjoyable and insightful process. If you have taken one, do another one and study it more closely this time. There are many good personality assessments available, but the simplest and most powerful one I have found is based on the DISC model. There are four dominant personality types and many combinations. In the DISC model, the D's are the people who are risk-takers, decisive, goal-oriented, and dominant. The I's are the funny, inspirational people who love to laugh and make others laugh with them. The S's are the safe, secure, faithful, hardworking, and sincere people you can count on. The C's are the calculated, precise, exact, planning people of our society.

Here's an example of each personality: Imagine a house needs to be renovated. A D would say something like, "Okay, we need to knock down this wall and tear those pipes out over there. C'mon, let's get this done." And I would say, "I'll get the pizza and bring the music. Who's going to be there?" An S would say, "Where do you need me? Just tell me what to do." They'll also be the last one there at 10:00 at night, with a flashlight, painting the final corner of a room. A C would say, "Uh, do we have permits for all of this?"

You can probably identify yourself as a D, I, S, or C from that illustration. Each personality type has its strengths and weaknesses, and learning yours and those of others is critical to becoming successful. We all have different needs. Learning more about who you are and what meets your needs allows you to consciously engage in work that fulfills you. Learning the other personality types allows you to identify other people. When you can identify someone's personality, you're able to speak their language and better meet their needs. When you can speak someone's language and meet their needs, you become a leader. Entrepreneurs understand themselves and others. Do you know

> Successful entrepreneurs know their own strengths and weaknesses.

what drives you? Successful entrepreneurs know their own strengths and weaknesses. People who do not know their strengths and weaknesses will always need to be managed and told what to do. But people who develop self-insight and learn to understand and connect with others can become successful entrepreneurs.

One of the skills of great entrepreneurs is the ability to network or build relationships. Granted, networking does seem to come easier for some people than others, but regardless of personality, anyone can learn to build good relationships.

We've all heard the old saying "It's not what you know, it's who you know." There is some truth to that, but a more accurate statement would be, "It's who and what you know." Entrepreneurs continually improve their networking skills. They make it a priority to increase their knowledge about the people they want to network with. Who do you want to connect with? How much do you know about their interests? Educating yourself about the interests of someone you want to build a relationship with is critical. If there is no common ground, then chances are you won't build a relationship.

So my advice for those who want to become successful entrepreneurs is to start with educating yourself about yourself and then learn how to build better relationships.

Another important subject in a successful entrepreneur's education is leadership. Entrepreneurship and leadership go hand in hand. Leadership is influence. Successful entrepreneurs are those who have learned how to influence others. Unsuccessful entrepreneurs are those who have not yet learned how to lead. You must study and practice the principles of leadership if you want to become a successful entrepreneur. Although there are many principles of leadership, I will just share what I believe to be two of the most important ones here: As I have continued to educate myself and experience entrepreneurial successes and fail-

> Leadership is influence. Successful entrepreneurs are those who have learned how to influence others.

ures, it has become abundantly clear that you must learn to inspire and encourage yourself and others.

Inspiration . . .

Inspiration is the result of a positive belief in yourself, in people, in opportunities, and in the work you're engaged in. It comes from thinking about entrepreneurial endeavors with a positive attitude, that you can and will succeed. One of the secrets to being able to inspire others is you must be able to keep yourself inspired. True leadership starts with self-leadership. If you can't keep yourself inspired, then you can't inspire others very well. Inspiration helps entrepreneurs to stay focused on their goals and consistently take action toward them. Successful entrepreneurs are able to stay focused and keep taking action because they believe that what they are doing is important, not only for themselves but also for others. True leaders inspire others to believe they can achieve their goals and that their goals are meaningful and important to others as well. Everyone enjoys being part of something important, something meaningful, something bigger than themselves. It becomes much easier for you to inspire others if you are engaged in work that is important to you and makes a positive difference in the lives of other people.

Successful entrepreneurs inspire others to believe that their products and services are so important that a person's life will be better off because of them. If you truly believe in what you are doing and promoting, then the power of inspiration will help carry you through the inevitable tough times, struggles, and failures. Without inspiration, it's extremely difficult to achieve success. Success requires work, lots of work, and it's inspiration that empowers you to keep working when you feel like giving up. Einstein once said that genius is 1 percent inspiration and 99 percent perspiration. I would like to add that it is the 1 percent of inspiration that makes the 99 percent perspiration possible. People will not work very long or hard to accomplish a significant goal unless they are truly inspired to do so. If you practice keeping yourself inspired, you'll be educating yourself on how to inspire others. It's when entrepreneurs can keep themselves and others inspired that they create more success.

Encouragement . . .

Encouragement is closely linked to inspiration. In fact, they often feed and support each other. But there are some small distinctions between the two. Here's a few of the key differences between inspiration and encouragement: Inspiration usually helps people get started, whereas encouragement usually helps people keep going. Inspiration is more an internal feeling and encouragement is more an external action, whether it is a simple smile, a pat on the back, or one sincere sentence that tells someone they can do it or that they can get back on track when they've had a setback. Some of the most meaningful encouragement is given through our words. Sometimes communicating to someone that you have faith in them and believe they can succeed is all they need to actually succeed. Many, many people fail because of a lack of encouragement in their lives. Many more people would have achieved many more successes in their lives if they had encouragement to do so.

> Encouragement can change someone's attitude, which will change their actions, which will change their results.

Don't let this simple truth slip past you here. Encouragement can change someone's attitude, which will change their actions, which will change their results. Encouragement changes everything, and if you make it a regular, even daily, part of your life, you will reap huge benefits.

As with inspiration, if you can't keep yourself encouraged then it is impossible to encourage others. The role encouragement plays in the life of an entrepreneur cannot be overstated. Encouragement is so vital because we all get discouraged at times, especially when things don't work out according to our plans. Discouragement is an enemy of success. If you can learn to encourage yourself and others, then you will persevere and overcome the obstacles that get in your way. Don't wait to encourage someone. Do it today and do it as much as you can. Don't wait for someone to encourage you, learn to encourage yourself. Successful entrepreneurs get good at encouraging others because they practice on themselves so much. When you find yourself discouraged, it is your responsibility to encourage yourself and get back to taking action toward your goals. Being discouraged simply means you have lost your focus or changed your focus from what is truly important to you and are focusing on something or someone that is hindering your progress and success. One of the best ways to get back to feeling encouraged is to *refocus on your highest priorities.* We all lose our focus sometimes, and when we do, it is always our responsibility to refocus. Refocusing is often the difference between entrepreneurial success and failure. When you lose your focus, learn to refocus. When you learn to consistently refocus your mind and efforts on what's most important to you, you will keep yourself encouraged and be able to encourage others. Educate yourself about leadership. Learn to lead with inspiration and encouragement. Leading through inspiration and encouragement creates successful entrepreneurs.

Entrepreneurs educate themselves more than they entertain themselves.

Employees entertain themselves more than they educate themselves.

Entrepreneurs have an empowering perspective of failure.

Employees see failure as bad.

Several years ago I saw a building for lease in my hometown. It was a double drive-thru on the corner of the second-busiest intersection in the city, and I thought it would make a great coffee and smoothie store. I began researching franchises, and after finding a partner to manage the day-to-day operations, we started the process of opening the store.

As with most things in life, it didn't go exactly

according to plan. We thought the store would be up and running within three to four months but we were met with delay after delay, which translated into expense after expense. In the end, we didn't open our doors for eight months. It took more than twice as long as we had anticipated, and drained twice as much capital.

The problems didn't end there. There were more setbacks after opening, and the store quickly went into the red and stayed there until I finally decided to close it some eighteen months later. I had invested $250,000 to get the store up and running and had to pay an additional $50,000 to pay off the building lease and equipment leases in order to close it down. All told, I lost over $300,000 and enormous amounts of my time. It was not a fun season. Educational, yes; fun, no!

I spent many months blaming my partner and finding fault, focusing on the things he did wrong. But after some deep soul-searching, I finally realized that I had to take responsibility for my results. All of them. So I embraced the failure and began to learn some valuable lessons.

Failure Is Feedback

Our traditional school system trains children to close their books and not ask for help at test time. It grades them on a scale from pass to fail. Along the way, it also trains kids to believe that failure is bad. In reality, failure is simply feedback. Failure is the way we learn and grow. It shows us where there needs to be a correction. For most people, however, failure is not correction but rejection.

> Failure is the way we learn and grow. It shows us where there needs to be a correction.

Never take failure personally. One belief I have that has served me well is that *failure* is a verb, not a noun. Failure is just something you do—it's not something you are. We have all failed many times and we will fail again. It's part of life. Failure is the opportunity to begin again in a new and better way. Successful entrepreneurs believe failure is inevitable and educational.

The lessons that you can gain from failure are more precious and powerful than any you can learn from reading a book. Failure is feedback from the real world, and one of the first benefits that you can gain from that feedback is the knowledge that you took action. If you're not experiencing failure then you probably aren't taking risks. Be proud of yourself when you fail because it means you took action. You created a result. You made an impact on the world. Take solace in the fact that, positive or negative, you made a difference through your own actions and created an experience you could learn from.

Next, ask yourself, "What is the most important lesson I can learn from this failure?" There is usually one key lesson that each failure can teach us, and other smaller lessons can be learned as well. Learn to squeeze your failures for lessons like oranges for juice. Get everything out of them that you can.

As my coffee shop business began to unravel, I took 50 percent responsibility for the failure and blamed my partner for the other half. It seemed logical—after all, we were partners. But after some time I still felt angry and somewhat depressed about the failure, so I decided to take more responsibility. "All right," I said, "I take 75 percent responsibility. Only 25 percent of the failure is his fault." I felt a little better about that, but deep down I was still angry. Nearly a year after closing the business I was walking with my wife and I said to her, "You know, I think I am finally at the place where I can take 90 percent responsibility for that failure."

My wife, God bless her, said, "Well, when you can take 100 percent responsibility for it, then you'll get over it."

I was speechless (which doesn't happen very often). How dare she? I was a little angry, but deep down I knew she was right, and I did what I had to: I accepted it. At that moment I took 100 percent responsibility, and instantly something amazing and mysterious happened: an invisible weight lifted off of me. I felt an increase in energy and a sense of freedom and happiness that I had not felt in a while.

Throughout the year after the failure I kept asking myself, "What can I learn from this?" The answers didn't come quickly because deep down I was still angry and blaming my partner for the failure, and as long as I blamed and complained, I remained the same. This is an important lesson to learn: As long as you blame and complain, you remain the same. But when you take 100 percent responsibility for your results you begin to see many valuable lessons in your failures. There are two main lessons I learned when I stopped blaming my partner for the failure of the coffee shop.

The first was to take responsibility—100 percent of it. It was my money and my choice to take the risk to open the store. It was my choice who I asked to be my partner.

I made the choice to give my partner a great deal of control in that business. In fairness to him, I now believe he did the best he could under the circumstances. His previous experience was not in entrepreneurial situations, and his background did not equip him for what I wanted him to do. With the benefit of hindsight, I can say now that I wish he had communicated better, persevered longer, and learned how to make the business more profitable, but ultimately none of that matters.

Entrepreneurs must take responsibility for their failures. They can't blame, complain, and justify if they are to learn from failure and use it

> Entrepreneurs must take responsibility for their failures.

to become better, stronger, and wiser. Entrepreneurs must seek and find the answers they need. It does no good to stay angry and blame others for a failure after it has happened. Entrepreneurs must learn to detach from blame.

Employees can blame, complain, and quit when things get hard. Entrepreneurs must stay strong and choose to get stronger during the failures of life. Those failures may not be easy, but as you learn to accept them and learn from them, you'll become stronger and more confident.

The second powerful lesson I learned from the failure was to learn to communicate better. I had to take responsibility for not communicating well enough. I failed to communicate my expectations clearly to my partner, and he failed to communicate with me. Many failures occur due to misunderstandings, and misunderstandings are simply the result of poor communication.

Open, honest communication is a skill that good entrepreneurs continually develop. Failure to communicate leads to more failure. Learning to communicate leads to success. We learn by practice, and you need to practice communicating every day.

Successful entrepreneurs constantly cultivate their ability to communicate. Learning to clearly communicate a message so others can easily understand it is a skill you can develop. It is a skill that almost all top income earners have practiced and polished. Clear communication comes from clear thinking. If your thinking is not clear then it is very difficult to communicate a clear message. Having a clear vision in your mind helps your mouth communicate it more clearly. Some people find it easier to communicate their thoughts than others do. These people are often referred to as "gifted communicators," but even if they do not consider themselves as such, they can learn to be if they will commit to it. Communicating is just as much a learned skill as it is a gift or talent.

Communication is another one of those subjects that aspiring entrepreneurs must study and practice. Many failures in business and our personal life can be traced back to a failure to communicate clearly—or worse, a failure to communicate at all. For great insights on effective communication, I recommend a book written by my mentor Nido Qubein, *How to Be a Great Communicator.*

Failure is simply a part of life, especially the life of someone learning to be a successful entrepreneur. Always remember, failure is not your enemy. Failure is your friend. It's one of life's many teachers, and when you begin to see failure as a positive, you'll also begin seeing the benefits it offers you. You will not—in fact, you cannot—see the benefits of failure as long as you perceive it as negative. Believe that it is good and you will learn and grow. Unsuccessful employees

see failure as bad and that perspective leaves
them powerless to achieve true success. Your
perspectives produce
your results. If you
want the result called
Success, then you must
work on developing an
empowering perspective of failure. The most
successful entrepreneurs I know have failed
many, many times. I have failed many times, but
the lessons learned from my failures have played
a vital role in the successes I have achieved. If
you will look for lessons from your failures, you
will discover that they will teach you exactly
what you need to succeed.

> Always remember,
> failure is not your
> enemy. Failure is your
> friend.

*Entrepreneurs have an empowering
perspective of failure.*

Employees see failure as bad.

8

Entrepreneurs are solution finders.

Employees are problem solvers.

Have you ever spent time "solving a problem" only to have to solve the same problem again in a few days, weeks, or months?
When you "solve" problems, what you're really
doing is seeking a quick fix so you can get back
to a familiar routine. When you "find solutions,"
however, you fix a problem so that it won't be a
problem again.

Problem solvers are nearsighted. They don't

think in terms of trying to eliminate problems so they don't reoccur. Employees tend to be problem solvers. When a problem arises that wasn't covered in their training, they don't believe it's their responsibility to fix it. Entrepreneurs, on the other hand, know that when a problem arises it's their responsibility to find a solution so they don't have to waste time and money with it in the future. Successful entrepreneurs always seek to solve a problem permanently, or to find a long-term solution.

> Successful entrepreneurs always seek to solve a problem permanently, or to find a long-term solution.

Solution-finding is more difficult than problem-solving because it requires you to keep seeking a solution until you find one. One of the key distinctions between problem solvers and solution finders is the amount of time each will give to seeking a solution. An employee with the problem solver mentality will only seek a solu-

tion for a short time and then pass the responsibility on to someone else. Then someone else has
to stop what they are doing and listen to the
problem and "try" to solve it.

If that person also has the problem solver
mentality, they will also "try" to solve it, and if
they can't quickly do so, they'll pass it on to
someone else.

This can be a terrible time-wasting cycle. At
some point, someone may finally solve the problem temporarily. If they haven't found a solution, however, the next time the problem arises
the vicious time-wasting cycle begins again.

Developing the solution finder mentality requires a commitment to do whatever it takes,
and to "keep on keeping on" until a solution is
found. Solution finders are tenacious, and take
personal responsibility for problems. While unsuccessful employees often say, "It's not my
problem," becoming a successful entrepreneur
requires embracing problems and taking respon-

sibility for finding long-term solutions. Unsuccessful employees will use the excuse that it's
"not my problem" when they don't know how
to solve it, or maybe they are just unwilling to
put forth the effort necessary to find a solution.
Successful entrepreneurs operate from a mind-set
that says, "Even though I don't know how to
solve this problem right now, I can figure it out,
and I will find a solution no matter how long it
takes or how hard it is." Entrepreneurs are willing to work hard to find solutions because they
value time. They do not want to have to waste
time in the future. Many employees who get
paid by the hour really don't care about saving
time down the road because they believe they are
going to get paid the same anyway. In reality,
many entrepreneurs or CEOs would gladly com-
pensate their employees who find solutions that
help the company save time. Successful entrepreneurs understand that time is money. If they can
invest a little more time and work harder now to

find a solution to a problem that will save a lot more time later, then it's well worth the extra time and work to do so. Finding solutions saves time and money. Temporary problem-solving ends up wasting time and money.

The differences between the solution finder mentality and the problem solver mentality can be applied to two main areas: personal problems and professional problems.

Personal Problems

Your habits create your life. Your personal problems and your successes are directly related to your daily habits. Both conscious and unconscious patterns of thought and action are responsible for the results you create. If you continually

> Success and failure in almost any endeavor can be traced back to your daily routine.

have personal problems, then don't look at others—look no further than your habits, especially your daily habits. Success and failure in almost any endeavor can be traced back to your daily routine.

Realize, too, that there are things you are in the habit of doing and there are things you are in the habit of not doing. Most people think that habits are only about what they do, but the things you don't do are just as important. In fact, a very simple and powerful formula for success is to do more of the things that get you closer to your goals and less of the things that keep you from them.

Your daily routine either creates or eliminates personal problems. If you're not making progress toward success, take a close look at the things you do every day, your habits, and see what needs to change. It's not an accident that so many people experience the same old problems over and over again—it's an example of habits at work.

Temporarily changing your actions is just problem-solving. Permanently changing your habits is solution-finding. Solution finders develop habits that eliminate many of their personal problems. They're committed to working on their mind-set and actions until they consistently get the results they want. Changing our habits is not easy. If it were easy, then everyone would be successful and fulfilled. Successful entrepreneurs are willing to do what's hard in their personal and professional lives in order to achieve positive results. Doing what's hard could be referred to as *discipline*. Daily discipline done over time creates positive habits that make life easier by eliminating many problems. Daily disciplines create and maintain solutions for your life and business. Daily disorders create and multiply problems in your life and business. In our personal lives the word to find solutions to our problems is *discipline,* in our professional lives the word to find solutions is *system*. You can say that your daily disciplines are the system for running your personal life smoothly. If your personal life is experiencing stormy seas instead of smooth sailing, then daily disciplines will help you create positive habits that will calm the storm, or find solutions, so you can enjoy your journey.

Professional Problems

Most professional problems are the result of system failure not people failure. A small business, private practice, franchise, Fortune 500 company, or any other business must develop systems if it wants to reduce problems and be more productive. Solution finders work on developing systems that produce consistent results. You may have heard the acronym SYSTEM: Save Yourself Stress Time Energy and Money. To find solutions for problems that keep coming up over and over again you must create a system.

Once a system is created it must be operated consistently. If you create a system and see better results, then you are making progress. If you create a system and still have the same old problems, then you go back to the drawing board.

Notice I use the word *create*. However, you may be in a job or career where you have a system that simply needs to be updated. If you are a boss who is enforcing a system for your company and new problems start to come up, don't immediately blame the people, look at the system and see if it needs to be updated. If you are an employee who is following a system at work and see a way to improve it, then do it. That just may be your ticket from employee to boss. If you have some problems that have been around for a while, then you need to create a system. If your business has experienced smooth sailing for a season and then new problems start cropping up, you need to update the system. Solution finders create and update systems. The beauty of a good system is that it provides long-term, not short-term, solutions to problems. Learn to create and update systems, and you'll discover the essence of solution-finding for professional problems.

Successful entrepreneurs understand that their personal and professional lives affect and influence each other and that finding solutions in one will help them find solutions in the other. If you commit to developing daily disciplines in your personal life, it will also help you create and update systems in your professional life, and vice versa. The reason is because disciplines and systems help create peace of mind. Peace of mind is a powerful state that allows creativity to flow. The more peace you can create at home, the more powerful and creative you'll be in finding solutions for problems at work; the more peace you create at work, the more powerful and creative you'll be in finding solutions for problems at home. Developing disciplines and creating systems are not easy, but after they are in place the rewards and benefits are well worth the efforts. Successful entrepreneurs are willing to do what's hard now to make life easier later. Unsuc-

> Successful entrepreneurs are willing to do what's hard now to make life easier later.

cessful employees do what's easiest now and end up making things harder later. Develop a solution finder mentality and do what may be hard for a little while. Your long-term results will make you smile.

Entrepreneurs are solution finders.

Employees are problem solvers.

7

Entrepreneurs know a little about a lot.

Employees know a lot about a little.

I once heard a story about a CEO who was having a meeting with someone from outside of
his company. During the meeting an employee
burst in and said, "We've got a problem. We've
got to handle this right now!"

The CEO calmly looked at the employee and
said, "Remember rule number 5."

The employee thought for a second and then
smiled, relaxed, and said, "Right—rule number

5. Thank you," and then turned and walked out of the room. The CEO resumed his conversation and within minutes another employee came running in and said, "Something has just come up that requires your immediate attention."

Once again the CEO calmly looked at the employee and said, "Remember rule number 5."

The employee visibly relaxed and said, "Oh yeah—rule number 5. Sorry, I forgot." Then he smiled and walked out of the room.

At this point, the visitor thought to himself, *Wow, I've never seen anything like that before. I've got to find out what rule number 5 is.* Once again the CEO resumed his conversation and once again he was interrupted by yet another employee with an urgent cry for help. The CEO reminded the worker of rule number 5, with the same calming result.

Finally, the visitor couldn't take it any longer. "I've never seen anything like that," he exclaimed. "What in the world is rule number 5?"

The CEO smiled and said, "Rule number 5 is 'Don't take yourself so damn seriously.' "

The visitor asked, "How many rules are there?"

The CEO gave an even bigger smile and said, "Just one."

The moral of the story is that things are rarely as serious as they may first appear. While inexperienced entrepreneurs may run around trying to put out fires, a more seasoned entrepreneur will let many fires just burn themselves out. Why? Because entrepreneurs know a little about a lot, and this broader, more generalized view allows them to see what's truly important and keep things in a more balanced perspective. Entrepreneurs can see the big picture, while employees can only see their small piece of the puzzle. Employees tend to think the

> Entrepreneurs can see the big picture, while employees can only see their small piece of the puzzle.

thing they know about is much more serious than it really is because it's all they know. Knowing a lot about a little can make you think your part is more important than it is. Knowing a little about a lot makes you realize that although everyone's role is important, no one role is so serious that it means success or failure in and of itself.

As an entrepreneur I have had to understand schedules, ordering, fulfillment, human relations, risk management, billing, shipping, returns, insurance, advertising, marketing, customer service, payroll, taxes, legal matters, income and expenses, hiring and firing, and more! During my employee days, all I had to do was show up and stick to my job description. If you want to remain an employee for the rest of your life then just stick to your job description and don't worry about learning about anything else. On the other hand, if you want to become an entrepreneur, then you must develop an interest in the big picture, and how things work together. It is wise to learn a little about a lot.

It takes a conscious effort to learn about the many facets of running a company—as an entrepreneur, there is always something that seems to be demanding your attention. It takes time to learn about the many things you need to know to become a successful entrepreneur. I have been an entrepreneur for twenty years now and I am still learning new things. Having to know about so much can be overwhelming if you let it, but if you stay focused on the big picture and learn to delegate the smaller things, you will experience more success and less stress.

If something goes wrong for an employee, they tend to think it's the end of their world. It's not. It never is. Life and business always go on. If you decide to learn more about the big picture it will help you keep things in a proper perspective. Things are usually not as serious as they first appear. Whatever challenge arises, it's likely not the end of the world. Entrepreneurs understand that things go wrong and don't worry too much when they do. They just calmly handle the matter at hand and keep moving forward with the big picture in mind.

In my early twenties I was a golf apprentice at a prestigious golf course. I clearly remember having an enlightening conversation with the head pro about quitting my job to take another one for better pay. I told him that I wanted to start the new job immediately, but didn't want to leave with no one to cover my schedule. Instead, I offered to give him longer than two weeks' notice before leaving, if he needed it. I can remember him smiling gently and saying, "Keith, please don't take this the wrong way, but if, God forbid, you left here tonight and got in a car accident and couldn't come to work tomorrow, this place would go right on without you. So you can leave whenever you're ready."

My employee mentality got rocked. I thought my role was such an important part of the team, and that leaving was "serious." I quickly discovered that for a seasoned entrepreneur with a broad perspective, many things just aren't that serious.

The way you learn a little about a lot is simply to keep expanding your mind. By continually learning new things about different facets of business you gain a clearer picture of the big picture. Clarity helps you maintain a powerful perspective so that when a problem or failure occurs you are ready to handle it. Knowing a little about a lot allows you to more quickly and easily find solutions when problems arise. The less knowledge you have, the bigger problems will appear to you and it will be harder to find a solution. Knowing a little about a lot allows you to

> Knowing a little about a lot allows you to more quickly and easily find solutions when problems arise.

look at many problems and say, "That's no big deal. Here's what we are going to do about it." But when your knowledge is limited to only one or two main things, you often say, "What are we going to do about this problem?" People who don't consistently increase their knowledge will always have low limits on the success they can achieve.

I'll finish this Distinction by sharing four of the many things that most successful entrepreneurs know a little about. I learned them from my friend Glen Kaplan, who is the CEO of ChargeToday.com. He has been a successful entrepreneur for the last twenty years. The four things can easily be remembered with the acronym SODA: Simplification, Organization, Delegation, and Automation. These are four of the many things you absolutely must know a little about to become a successful entrepreneur. The time, energy, and money that you spend learning

about these four things will be well invested because they will help you experience more successes and less failures.

Entrepreneurs know a little about a lot.

Employees know a lot about a little.

Entrepreneurs give and receive praise and correction.

Employees don't praise, and try to avoid correction.

My son's karate teacher uses a powerful tool to get the best from his students and himself. It's called "PCP," which stands for Praise, Correct, Praise.

Rather than criticizing or correcting errors immediately, when the instructor spots a mistake during a student's training, he uses the PCP strategy to get better results, first praising or complimenting the student on what he did right, then correcting the mistake, and then praising the improvement.

Take a kick, for instance. If a child halfheartedly kicks his leg instead of kicking with force, the instructor might say, "Great, excellent, you got your leg moving in the right direction. Now let's do it with more strength." When the child kicks harder, the instructor gives him a high five and says, "That's it, good job!" Praise, then correct, then praise again.

Not only is it great for kids, it works exceptionally well for adults, too—in my experience adults aren't much different when it comes to being corrected. Have you ever heard the old saying that a spoonful of sugar helps the medicine go down? Praise is like sugar, correction is like medicine. Adults enjoy being praised just as much as children do, and praising people is a key secret of success. Successful entrepreneurs have learned to praise before they correct, and then praise again when they see improvement.

Entrepreneurs understand that correction is not rejection, and as an entrepreneur it's important to help employees feel safe enough to offer suggestions and even corrections. Many employees try to avoid correction because they take it personally and feel rejected. While correction on its own can often be misunderstood as a personal attack, PCP helps people feel accepted and encouraged.

Entrepreneurs practice not taking things personally. We understand that people act and speak out of their own mental and emotional conditioning, and that a personal attack usually has little to do with us and more to do with the person attacking. If someone appears to be attacking you, just remember that's who they have been taught to be. Don't take it personally.

From Corrections to Solutions

Not only do successful entrepreneurs use PCP with their employees, they also teach their employees to use PCP when communicating with *them*. Entrepreneurs appreciate an employee offering a solution when they see something or someone that needs to be corrected. A true correction is seeing and communicating about something that's not working and then offering a possible way to resolve it. If someone only points out what's wrong without offering a solution, then all they are really doing is complaining, and successful entrepreneurs hate complaining. I imagine many employees have felt like their boss was complaining about something because they don't understand that continual correction is absolutely necessary to keep a company on track. Like driving a car or flying an airplane, the driver or pilot must make hundreds, even thousands of small corrections in order to stay on track and eventually arrive at their destination. Without corrections there is no such thing as success.

Running a successful company demands that you make many corrections. As long as you are using PCP, your corrections will rarely be received as a complaint. Now, I do know average and below average entrepreneurs who complain a lot, and their complaining has run off some good employees and customers because they didn't understand the destructive power of it. Also, I imagine that millions of employees have lost their jobs because they were whiners. Whether you are an entrepreneur or an employee, complaining causes you to lose, correcting causes you to win. Complaining creates problems, it doesn't solve them. So practice using PCP to make sure that you aren't just complaining and creating problems for yourself. As an entrepreneur I understand that solutions create successes, so I choose to praise people before offering a correction so that there will be a spirit of cooperation instead of conflict. Once someone perceives something you say as a complaint instead

> Complaining creates problems, it doesn't solve them.

of a sincere correction, it is very easy to allow the conversation to escalate into a fight. At the least, complaining can create resentment, but sincere compliments before corrections allow a mutual respect to remain present. If you'd like to operate your business with more respect and less resentment among people, get good at PCP. If the word *praise* doesn't resonate with you, then call it The C3 Strategy: Compliment, Correct, Compliment. People love to be complimented! Complimenting creates cooperation, and cooperation allows people to work together smoothly and find solutions. Praise, or complimenting, is a very simple and powerful strategy to help you create more success and enjoy the process more because there is less stress and more peace between people, and that's always a wonderful thing.

Receiving Correction

Accepting and using correction requires one simple virtue: humility. Humility provides the ability to learn and grow. It's the willingness to consider what someone else is saying. Arrogant entrepreneurs and employees forfeit their power and potential by being unwilling to consider someone else's point of view. There is power in humility, and learning to consider views different from your own allows you to tap into that power.

Many people believe that by practicing humility, they will be taken advantage of. In my experience, the opposite is true: Humility is power, not weakness. Arrogance is weakness, and has led to many failures. The art of humility is beautiful. It draws out the good in others, and creates a mosaic of ideas that can create great success.

> Arrogance is weakness, and has led to many failures. The art of humility is beautiful.

One of the greatest benefits of humility is that it helps develop the ability to listen without interrupting. When you learn to simply listen without interruption, you go beyond communicating with people to connecting with them. It is wisdom to try and connect with someone before you correct them, and PCP helps you do that. Connect before you correct. And when you're the one being corrected, simply show some respect by listening to understand the other person's perspective. When you're being corrected, the natural tendency is to defend yourself, but the mature thing to do is to remain silent and show respect for the other person by letting them finish what they're saying and sincerely trying to see their point of view.

Humility is also the ability to take responsibility and not blame others. Many corrections are really just the blame game in disguise. Blaming never accomplishes anything constructive. As you practice the art of humility, become conscious of correcting with a solution instead of just blaming. If you've ever watched the TV show *The Apprentice*, you've seen some great examples of blamers and complainers. Most of the young people on the show refuse to take responsibility and always point the finger. There's nothing wrong with saying, "I was wrong, I screwed up, I'm sorry." By acknowledging your mistakes in this way, you quickly earn the respect of others. We all screw up. By blaming, you remain the same and make it very difficult to develop relationships that are vital to your success.

The next time you need to give a correction, be sure to include some sincere praise and really connect with the person. And the next time you are receiving a correction, practice some humility and do your best to give them sincere respect.

Entrepreneurs give and receive praise and correction.

Employees don't praise, and try to avoid correction.

**Entrepreneurs say,
"The buck stops here."**

Employees say, "It's not my fault."

Learning to take personal responsibility is a common theme throughout this book and my others. The path to becoming a great entrepreneur begins with first learning to take responsibility for your personal life. As you learn to take responsibility for your own life, you will also be learning how to take responsibility for a company.

Every day you're given a choice: You can either take responsibility, or you can blame, complain, and justify. Blaming, complaining, and justifying are simply excuses for why you can't be, do, or have what you want. It is impossible to take responsibility for your life while you are blaming, complaining, and justifying.

Part of taking responsibility is accepting what is. Most people waste enormous amounts of energy by resisting it. What is, is. Wishing things were different will not change the facts. While many people sit around and wish this or that would happen, responsible people get off their

> Taking responsibility means working toward making things better.

butts and go make things happen. Accepting what is doesn't mean leaving things as they are, it means acknowledging the way they are. Taking responsibility means working toward making things better. "The buck stops here" means acknowledging things as they are and taking action to make them better. Taking responsibility means staying focused and taking consistent action toward your goals.

It requires more energy to sit around and blame, complain, and justify than it does to take action, even massive action. You would think that taking massive action would make you tired, but in reality when you take action toward a goal, it energizes you. It's also important to realize that every area of life is connected and what happens in one area affects the others. Have you noticed that when you exercise you feel better mentally and emotionally? Have you noticed that when you are down emotionally it affects the way you feel physically? Have you noticed that when you focus your mental energy on your goals or reflect on something that you are thankful for, it makes you feel better physically and emotionally? Taking responsibility to manage your energy is one of the most important things you can do.

When you blame, complain, and justify, you

lower your energy. When you take positive actions toward your goals, you increase your energy and build positive momentum. If you've ever been caught in a downward spiral where things seemed to be getting worse and worse, it's very likely that you were complaining, blaming, or justifying.

Taking responsibility means you refuse to play the blame game. Taking responsibility means you refuse to complain and justify. By focusing on your goals and taking consistent action toward them you are in essence saying, "The buck stops here, my successes and my failures are my responsibility." When you give up all complaining, blaming, and justifying and focus on taking consistent action, you will be amazed at how much you accomplish.

> Taking responsibility means you refuse to play the blame game. Taking responsibility means you refuse to complain and justify.

One of the most important parts of taking responsibility is to measure your results. Entrepreneurs often stop and ask themselves: "Are my actions getting me closer to my goals?" Most people don't ask that very often. They just keep doing the same things over and over with a false hope that things will get better. How often do you acknowledge where you are and measure it compared to where you were? Are you making progress in your life? It can be challenging to know unless you stop and measure your results. Most people justify their negative results by blaming and complaining. Don't let that be you. Learn to take responsibility by accepting what is, managing your energy, taking consistent action toward your goals, and measuring your results.

When I give talks I often use the story of the little red wagon.

Imagine that someone is pulling along a little red wagon. It's quite a sight because the wagon is filled with crap, piled high and overflowing. You can smell the stench.

The wagon full of crap represents all of the excuses people have about their life. It's full of the stories and excuses for why they can't be, do, or have. It's their stories and excuses for why they are the way they are and why their life is the way it is.

Now imagine someone approaches them and says, "Your life is your responsibility. If you take responsibility for your results you can create a great life." The person with the wagon immediately becomes defensive and says, "What? You don't know me! I can't do that, I have all of this crap in my life!"

We all have our stories, our crap, and we can take responsibility and let go of the little red wagon and move on, or we can blame, complain, justify, and stay the same. Some people have fooled themselves and they try to fool others into thinking that they are responsible, while continuing to hold on to the little red wagon. They may even get a can of gold spray paint and paint their crap gold. It may look better, but it still stinks! If your life stinks, then let go of the wagon. Stop blaming, complaining, and justifying, and start taking responsibility.

Whenever we complain, blame, or justify we are in essence saying, "It's not my fault." It's funny that we don't blame, complain, or justify our successes, just our failures or our actions that lead to failure. Whether someone blames their parents, the politicians, the corporations, their teachers or professors, sooner or later they have to take their eyes off others and look deep within their own hearts to see the truth. The truth is that our successes and failures are our own responsibility. Saying "The buck stops here" means you are willing to stop looking to others to make you successful and stop looking at them when you fail as if it were their fault. There's a very wise insight I learned from Jim Rohn; it's called "No Apology, No Complaint." The way he describes this philosophy is: If you reap a big harvest, you offer no apology. If you didn't receive much, you offer no complaint. I like to say it like this: If you create a great success, you offer no apology, and if you create a terrible failure, you offer no complaint. Jim says this philosophy is the highest form of wisdom. Whether you agree or not, you have to admit it's certainly a high level of maturity. A successful entrepreneur is a seasoned entrepreneur. The only way you mature is to experience many seasons of success and failure. Only a mature entrepreneur can say, "The buck stops here." Any immature employee can say, "It's not my fault." Enjoy your successes and endure your failures with an attitude of no apology, no complaint. Someone who is mature can endure; someone who isn't just blames, complains, and justifies.

Entrepreneurs say, "The buck stops here."

Employees say, "It's not my fault."

4

Entrepreneurs build wealth.

Employees make money.

Time flows constantly through our lives. It's impossible to create more of it, or get back what's already been used. Yet many people fail to realize that time is the most valuable asset they have. It's irreplaceable.

With that knowledge, consider for a moment how much time you exchange for money. Are you exchanging it wisely? We've all heard the statement "Time is money." A deeper revelation is that time is life, and when we waste time, we waste our lives.

Because of this relationship between time and life, it's important to value money. Make it a priority to learn to manage your money, because your money represents a portion of your life. When you frivolously spend your money on junk, you are, in a very real sense, wasting part of your life.

It's a common (and terrible) belief that money is not important. What's even more common is that people who hold that belief tend to be broke. If you don't value reading, then you probably don't have a library. If you don't value friendship, then you probably don't have any friends. If you don't value money, then you aren't likely to have any. We do not accumulate things that we do not value. What if I told my

> If you don't value money, then you aren't likely to have any. We do not accumulate things that we do not value.

wife she's not important to me? What if I told my kids they aren't important to me? What if I told my friends they're not important to me? Would they continue to hang around me? Of course not. Well, the same is true about your money.

If you say, "Money is not important to me," it's not going to hang around. From this day forward never say that money isn't important. It's one of the most destructive lies people tell themselves.

The Difference Between Money and Wealth

Since money is important, we should value it and learn to make it grow. But making money and making money grow are very different concepts; making money has very little in common with building wealth. You can make a lot of money, then spend it all and be broke. Yet you can make a smaller amount, learn to save and invest it, and build wealth. You can earn a million dollars a year, but it won't make you wealthy if you spend two million. Making money is a common mentality; building wealth is an uncommon mentality. Why are most people not wealthy in financial terms? Because their focus is on making money, not on building wealth.

Entrepreneurs focus on building wealth for themselves and the companies they work for. Learn to think about your life like a company— does your life show a profit at the end of the year, or did you spend everything you made? If a company lost money or never showed a profit year after year, it would close down, yet most people live their lives with no profit at the end of the year. Worse still, many people get deeper into debt with each passing year. The truth is that it's not their fault. This may sound shocking from someone who teaches personal responsibility, but most people with money management problems were never taught a better way. Our society doesn't teach children how to manage money and build wealth. How many college kids are given access to cash through credit cards, with absolutely no knowledge or experience of how to use them wisely? The fortunate few who were taught by their parents to build wealth should be extremely grateful. The rest of us—the vast majority who were not taught how to build wealth—must take personal responsibility for educating ourselves about making money grow.

Building wealth is the key to financial freedom, and this small shift in thinking toward "building wealth" instead of just "making money" can make a huge difference in your actions and the results you produce. Put and keep your focus on building wealth more than making money. Furthermore, make this distinction in your mind: Just as building wealth is not the same as making money, it's not the same as saving money, either. Saving $5,000 a year in an account that earns 3 percent interest while inflation is 3 percent isn't building wealth—it's breaking even.

Over the past two decades I've had many employees. I told each of them that I would help them in any way I could. Some of them were there just to get a paycheck and never asked for anything from me, but over time, some of them took me up on my offer.

One day, as I was about to leave for a vacation to Hawaii, two employees who were in their early twenties approached me and asked, "Keith, can you teach us how to make money?" I agreed, and asked each of them to go to a local bookstore while I was away, buy a certain book, and read it. Then, when I returned from vacation, we would discuss it.

While on vacation I was curious to see if they'd followed my instructions. When I returned to the office, I found out that both of them had bought the book but only one had actually read it. I invited the one who'd read it to my home so we could discuss it. He arrived right on time. I answered all his questions that evening and encouraged and challenged him to keep reading and learning.

A short time later he moved away; almost a year after that he called to tell me he was doing well, and had a great job he loved that paid $36,000 a year. He had only worked part-time for me and earned about $12,000 a year. In less than one year he'd tripled his income.

He also asked me to recommend another book to him, which I gladly did.

About ten months later he called again. He was talking fast and I could hear the excitement in his voice. He said, "Keith, I need another book. I got an incredible job and I need to learn how to invest my money so I can make it grow!" He informed me that he was now earning $1,000 a week.

In less than two years he had gone from earning $1,000 a month to $1,000 a week. When he first approached me he asked me to teach him how to "make money." Less than two years later he called and said he needed to learn how to "make it grow." He was ready to start building wealth. I never heard from him after that and often wonder how he is doing. I imagine he has gone through some failures and losses since embarking on the path of learning to build wealth, because that is part of the process, but I also suspect he's done quite well.

Don't fool yourself. If you are going to learn to build wealth you will experience some failures and losses. You may make money, and you may lose money—it's part of the process. Accept it, embrace it, learn from it, and stay focused on building wealth.

> If you are going to learn to build wealth you will experience some failures and losses. You may make money, and you may lose money—it's part of the process.

In *The Top 10 Distinctions Between Millionaires and the Middle Class* I wrote about three primary vehicles that many millionaires use to build wealth. They are real estate, stocks, and network marketing. Some people who have accumulated a fortune have used just one of these vehicles and many others have combined all three vehicles to build their wealth. There is no right or wrong number concerning how many vehicles you use to build wealth; it is an individual preference, so just do what is right for you. Some millionaires use just one vehicle to reach a wealthy lifestyle but when their wealth reaches a certain level (which is different for different people) they begin to seek and find more ways to make their money grow. In the beginning of your building-wealth journey, you and your small business will be the only things you have that are producing cash flow. And as you build your wealth you will probably want to find other vehicles to keep it growing. Just be sure to pick wealth-building vehicles that you enjoy learning about. Don't ever put your money into something that you have no knowledge of.

There are literally thousands of vehicles to help you build wealth, but I am only going to mention one more, which has a lot of different models to choose from. Some of them are some of the safest ways to build wealth; in fact, some people call them bulletproof. They are life insurance policies. Many life insurance policies are the safest investments because they usually have a lower rate of return than other vehicles and are not as risky as many others. But in the world of life insurance policies there are a lot of strategies to play the game. You can be as risky or as safe as you want to be. I recommend using the safer strategies to build wealth more slowly, and using a small business to build wealth more quickly. Some people advise you to use whole life policies and others teach people to buy term life policies and invest the difference. I am not going to advise you which way to go with life insurance policies, but I am advising you to learn about them and utilize them to build wealth.

Building wealth takes time; making money can be done quickly. Building wealth brings more security and certainty to your life and increases your peace of mind. Making money can stop at any moment and often has a lot of uncertainty and stress with it. Building wealth mostly comes from business. Making money mostly comes from a job.

The last thing I want to write about in this Distinction is simplicity. There is freedom in simplicity. The purpose of building wealth is to enjoy the true treasures of life, like your family and friends. While on your journey of building wealth it is wise to keep your lifestyle simple. There have been times in my life when our cost of living was relatively high, and there have been other times when we consciously chose to keep it low. Keeping our cost of living low always proved to be a simpler and much more peaceful way to live. Don't make the mistake or fall into the trap of complicating your life while trying to get rich. Don't even focus on getting rich. Focus on building wealth and you'll end up being rich with peace of mind. If you let it, life can become more complicated when you begin to build wealth. But if you value peace of mind and time with your family, keep things simple and enjoy the true treasures of life.

Entrepreneurs build wealth.

Employees make money.

3

Entrepreneurs fly with eagles.

Employees peck around with chickens.

I once had an excellent employee who started to slack on the job. The employee had always been a valuable asset to the company and seemed to really enjoy his work. I knew it was also the best-paying job he'd ever had, so I was very surprised when he started to flounder.

It was quite obvious to everyone that his poor job performance was directly related to his new girlfriend, but when I brought this to his attention, he claimed that his personal life had nothing to do with his professional life. I laughed and said, "You can't be serious." I waited for a response, but he just stared at me like a deer caught in the headlights. I explained to him that his personal and professional lives were intricately connected—that life at home affects your life at work, and vice versa. The people you choose to spend time with are some of the most important choices you make. "In essence," I told him, "you become like the people you spend time with. Period."

> The people you choose to spend time with are some of the most important choices you make.

Of course, he didn't see it that way. He felt he was still performing to the same standards he always had. Had he been honest with himself, though, he would have seen that he had started coming in late and was spending far too much time on the phone with her.

The worst part of it was how his normal, up-beat, positive energy had changed to being pes-simistic and tired. He seemed drained most of the time. His focus had shifted almost entirely to how he could please this girl. I had several talks with him, but he refused to see that his girlfriend had changed him. Needless to say, it was only a short time later that he was no longer working for me.

We parted on good terms and he even stopped by to say hi and ask me for advice on some jobs he was considering. He was a very likeable guy and he was quickly offered a posi-tion with another prestigious company. He told me he was going to take the job and seemed ex-cited about it.

About two weeks later he came by again and told me that instead of taking the previous offer, he was going to become licensed as an insurance adjuster and work with his brother. This shocked me. He'd never had anything positive to say about his brother—although he sincerely loved him, he was often frustrated by the life decisions his brother made.

When I asked him about the other position, he shrugged it off and said something about not wanting to work full-time, and that his brother had convinced him he could make twice as much in half the time by being an insurance adjuster. I couldn't help but wonder if wanting to spend more time with his girlfriend had influenced the decision. Nonetheless, I wished him well and told him to keep in touch.

A few weeks later I received a notice from the state requesting information about his work history. He had filed for unemployment. I never heard from him after that, although several months later I heard that he was back with the company he had worked for before coming to work for me, a place where he had never enjoyed the work or his coworkers.

What can you learn from his experience? The

people you spend time with influence your decisions and affect your energy. Like elevators, they either take you down or lift you up. The dangerous thing is that many people don't take the time to stop and ask how their relationships are affecting them. And since they don't ask that question, they don't see that the results they get are related to the relationships they're in.

You may not see an immediate effect from the people you spend time with, but over time they absolutely influence your life for the positive or the negative. The people you spend time with can make you, or they can break you. Think of your relationships like eyesight. When you first turn the lights off at night, it seems pitch black and at first

> The people you spend time with can make you, or they can break you.

you can't see anything. Then after a few minutes you begin to make out shapes in the room. Oh, there's the dresser. I think those are my shoes on the floor. I can see the outline of my chair. A few more minutes go by and it seems like someone must have turned a light on somewhere because now you can see the dresser, your shoes, and the chair clearly.

What has happened? There's no additional light in the room; your eyes have adjusted to the dark. And just like your eyes, you adjust to the environment of the people around you. Some people bring light into your life and help you see, while others bring darkness into your life and cause you to be blind. My old employee couldn't "see" that his new girlfriend was affecting him in a negative way on both a personal and professional level.

Many of your circumstances are a reflection of the expectations of the people you let influence your life. By choosing to invest your time with wise people who are living a life of success and significance, you learn to do the same. I have discovered that many people who are truly successful and fulfilled enjoy helping others achieve a more fulfilling life. Coaches and mentors are great, but I am not talking about a coach or mentor in this

> I have discovered that many people who are truly successful and fulfilled enjoy helping others achieve a more fulfilling life.

Distinction. I am talking about your personal relationships, especially the people you associate with on a regular basis.

Are you aware of how much time you spend with certain people, and are you aware of how they are influencing you? Hopefully you are aware of the positive and negative influences others have on you and are choosing to invest your time with the right people instead of wasting it with the wrong ones. Here are three great questions to ask yourself that I learned from Jim Rohn. Jim was a successful entrepreneur, motivational speaker, and business philosopher for several decades and touched the lives of millions of people. The three questions I learned from him can help you be more conscious, more aware, of the influences others have in your life, and empower you to be more proactive in developing better relationships.

What are my relationships doing to me?
Is that okay with me?
If not, then what am I going to do about it?

Have you ever stopped to ask yourself those questions, or some similar to them? Many people stay the same or get worse because they aren't willing to cut off certain people from their life. You don't get to choose who your family members are, but you absolutely do get to choose who your friends and colleagues are. The choices you make concerning the people you associate with on a consistent basis are some of the most important choices of your entire life. Are you

willing to let go of some people you've been
wasting your time with? Successful entrepreneurs invest their time with other successful people. Unsuccessful employees waste their time
with other unsuccessful people. *Successful* and
unsuccessful are relative terms, but this Distinction applies to each area of life, including your
finances. Consider this: It's very likely that your
income is the average of your five closest friends.
If you want to increase your income, then maybe
it's time to build some new relationships.

My mentor Nido Qubein is a successful entrepreneur, author, and professional speaker
who owns multiple companies. He had a very
wise mother. She told Nido, "Son, if you want to
be great then you must walk side by side and
hand in hand with great people. If you want to
be happy, then be around happy people. If you
want to be a drunk, then hang around drunks. If
you want to be rich, then find out what poor
people do and don't do that!"

If you want to learn the main reasons why some people become financially free and some don't, read *The Top 10 Distinctions Between Millionaires and the Middle Class.* I was able to write that book because I spent a lot of time with other millionaires before I became one. In addition to the multimillionaires I know who have ordered hundreds of copies of the book to give to friends and family, I have also had several millionaires who I didn't previously know contact me after they read the book to tell me how closely it matches how they think and feel.

I learned how to think like and become a millionaire by investing my time with millionaires. Before that I had learned how to be an entrepreneur by investing my time with entrepreneurs. Whoever and whatever you want to be, you must be around others who have already achieved it or are at least well on their way to achieving it. If you want to be a chicken, peck around with chickens. But if you want to be a successful entrepreneur, build relationships with successful entrepreneurs. The great thing about investing your time with eagles is, you will learn how to fly. The terrible thing about hanging around chickens is, you will eventually fry. Eagles fly and chickens fry. Which would you prefer? The choice is yours. Choose your relationships very carefully, for they will determine many of the things you experience in life.

Entrepreneurs fly with eagles.

Employees peck around with chickens.

2

Entrepreneurs look into the future.

Employees look into the past.

Few people understand the power of vision, and that's why most people are employees, not entrepreneurs. Very little of value happens without vision. A good marriage doesn't just happen without a vision to make it happen. Good health doesn't just happen without a vision to make it happen. Financial freedom doesn't just happen without a vision to make it happen. Vision makes things happen. All great entrepreneurs have vision. Vision is power. It's what attracts wisdom. It guides your life, and taking daily action toward your vision is the surest and fastest way to make it happen. You must create a vision of the future you desire if you are to experience success and fulfillment. Entrepreneurs make things happen because they have vision for the future. Employees watch things happen because they spend too much time in the past.

Great entrepreneurs use vision to create a balanced approach to productivity. We balance our time by planning for the future and taking action in the present. Most entrepreneurs spend very little time looking into the past. It's not that hindsight isn't important—it is, and can be used to develop good foresight—it's that we choose to put more of our emphasis on the future.

While it's important to value hindsight, don't let it limit your foresight—it's a mistake that many employees make. Looking into the past can help plan the future, but planning the future and taking action on that plan is the most important part. If you want to become more productive, then plan your work and work

> Don't spend excessive time looking into the past—it's a sure way to waste a lot of your present.

your plan. Don't spend excessive time looking into the past—it's a sure way to waste a lot of your present.

Sadly, most unsuccessful employees look into the past in order to complain, or they're haunted by regret, guilt, or shame. Looking into the past to wallow around in your pain will keep you stuck there, and doomed to repeat the same mistakes. Look into the past to see what you can learn and the pain will start to diminish. If you are living with guilt and shame, they will begin to lift. Learn from the past, and apply the lessons to your future.

When you look into the past to learn from it

you are standing in a powerful position called Responsibility. By looking into the past to learn, you are remaining present. Most employees are absent because they are still back there instead of here. And although entrepreneurs are sometimes absent, it's usually because they are dreaming of the future the way they want it to be.

Although dreaming of the future is much more powerful than dwelling on the past, it, too, can become a trap if you don't come out of your dream time and take action. Just thinking about something doesn't mean you are going to attract it. Remember this, a powerful vision is a goal accompanied by an action plan to achieve the goal. Thinking by itself will not make things happen. Thinking will start influencing your actions, but thoughts alone don't create success. Creating an action plan and then acting on it is far more powerful than thoughts alone. Success may start in your thoughts but it is accomplished by action.

Aligning Your Vision With That of Others

What is your vision? What's the vision of your company or the company you work for?

If your personal vision is not in alignment with the vision of your company or the company you work for, then it's time to look for another company. You will not be happy or fulfilled while working toward a vision you do not agree with. Your true success and happiness depends on you being true to your personal values. There are thousands of business opportunities and companies out there, and some of them are in alignment with your values—seek them out. People who love their jobs usually have personal visions that are very similar to the corporate vision of their employers.

> Your true success and happiness depends on you being true to your personal values.

Most people choose a career based on the

money they can make. As tempting as that seems, it's the worst way to choose a career. Find a career that is congruent with your personal values. If you've already chosen a career and made the mistake of choosing it based on income, then you may want to consider a change. You're not much of an asset to your company if you hate going to work, and that fact will eventually reveal itself—either in poor job performance, unhappiness, or both. On the other hand, if you find a company that supports your personal values, you'll be a valuable asset, someone who loves going to work and who creates an atmosphere of joy and peace.

Life is far too short to work a job that you hate. You may feel it's too late, that you've already been working for years on a job you don't like, but that only means that now, more than ever, it's time for a change. Stop wasting your precious time and energy and start investing it in a vision you believe in. When your work is congruent with your personal vision you become a valuable asset to your company. I use the phrase *your company* because employees who have personal visions that match their company's visions always personalize the company and act as if it is their own. If you've ever asked yourself how you can be a valuable asset to the company, start by making sure your visions are congruent, and then move from calling it *the* company to calling it *my* company. Entrepreneurs catch the vision of their company. They learn to clearly communicate it. They become it.

Entrepreneurs look into the future and plan how they can build wealth by building a great company. Employees look into the past and think they are entitled to promotions and raises because of seniority. To build a great company or to get promotions and raises you must fully embrace the vision of your company and run with it. Running means taking a lot of action or doing a lot of work. When you are running it is easier to stay focused and keep moving forward. When you are walking slow, or not taking much action, it is easy to get distracted and fall off the track. If your vision of the future is exciting, it compels you to run. It's much easier to work hard when you have a clear vision of a fulfilling future. If you lack vision and can't see life getting better for you, then distractions, disappointments, discouragements, and depression will be a constant part of your life. If you create a vision of a future that you'd love to experience and then start running toward it, the successes and failures, victories and defeats will give you a rich, rewarding life. The surest way to waste your life is to live it without a vision. The surest way to enjoy your life is to create a vision that inspires you, stay focused on it, and run with it. Choose where you want to go, take consistent steps in that direction, and work toward it relentlessly. Your future can be something you create or it can be something you hate. Look into the future through eyes of faith and see where you want to be five, ten, twenty, forty years from now. You don't have any more control over what you did or didn't do in the past, but you have complete control over what you do or don't do from this moment forward. The things you do and don't do will create the life you live in the future.

> The surest way to waste your life is to live it without a vision.

Look into the future and see where you want to go, then take consistent action toward that vision, and life will teach you through good and bad experiences everything you need to know to get there.

Entrepreneurs look into the future.

Employees look into the past.

1

Entrepreneurs take risks because of faith.

Employees play it safe because of fear.

In *The Top 10 Distinctions Between Million-aires and the Middle Class,* I wrote, "Risk is opportunity." When you take risk out of life, you take opportunity out of life. Many employees have taken opportunity out of their lives because they have more fear than faith. Successful entrepreneurs have strong faith, which allows them to find opportunities and take risks. Most people have little faith in themselves, and that's why they remain employees. Many employees say they would like to own their own business, but their fears keep them from taking the necessary risks.

Faith in Yourself

What you believe about yourself reveals itself in your performance. Do you have faith in yourself? If you look at your results and think they are not good enough, then I challenge you to look deeper for the reason why. The results you get are simply a reflection of what you are doing or not doing. And the things you are doing or not doing are simply the results of who you think you are.

If you think your results are not good enough, you may have a subconscious belief about yourself that says, "I am not good enough." And if you'll look a little deeper than that you may find a belief that says, simply, "I am not enough."

Are you enough? Of course you are! Entre-

preneurs believe in themselves. If you don't believe in yourself you will never find opportunities,
you'll never take the necessary risks, and you'll
never achieve the meaningful success you desire.
You must believe in yourself and cast out all
doubt. Self-doubt is the reason so many employees remain employees. Without faith in yourself
you will always need
someone else to tell
you what to do, or you
will look to others to
give you permission on

> Self-doubt is the
> reason so many
> employees remain
> employees.

what you can do. I believe the number one reason so many people remain employees is because
they are waiting for someone to give them permission to be something else.

If you don't have much faith in yourself, then
it's time to take the faith you do have and exercise it. Like a muscle, faith must be exercised to
grow and strengthen. You have faith. We all do.
The question is whether we are applying it.

Don't wait for someone else to give you permission to take action toward the lifestyle of success and significance that you desire.

Faith in Others

Faith in yourself empowers you to take risks. It also leads to having faith in others.

Do you have faith in others? Someone who disrespects others usually disrespects themselves. Someone who easily gets angry at others is easily angered by their own behavior. What you believe about yourself is projected onto others, and when you choose to believe in yourself, you'll find it easier to believe in others. You need people and people need you. By believing in yourself, others will sense that you believe in them, too. They will want to help you because they sense that you are sincere in wanting to help them.

When you have faith in yourself and others and you take risks together, you are more likely to succeed. A simple truth is, the more risks you take, the more likely it is you will meet with success. The fewer risks you take, the less likely you are to succeed. So take risks and take them with faith, believing in positive results. Risks taken in fear very often meet with failure.

> The fewer risks you take, the less likely you are to succeed.

Risk and Fear

You either choose to have faith, or you choose to be afraid. The number one reason people are afraid is because they believe things that aren't true. Perhaps you've heard the popular acronym for fear: FEAR—False Evidence Appearing Real.

In my Wisdom Creates Freedom workshop, I teach participants to use a powerful question to deal with fear. When faced with one of your fears, ask yourself, "What do I believe to be true that's not true?" As simple as this may sound, it works. The answer you get from that question will help identify the lie and reveal the truth about the situation. The truth will help you overcome your fear and strengthen your faith so you can take the necessary risks to succeed. Lies feed your fears and truth feeds your faith. Use this technique every time you face a fear. Your ego will want to justify your limiting beliefs but your heart knows the truth. If you are willing to listen to your heart and question your own beliefs, you will start experiencing more peace and joy. Peace and joy are powerful allies in a successful entrepreneur's life. They are the benefits of believing the truth.

Truth creates faith, lies create fear. Maybe you believe the lie that you are not enough. Maybe you believe the lie that it matters what someone else thinks about you. Maybe you believe a lie that you can't do it, whatever "it" may be. The lies you believe create the fears that keep you from taking the risks that can make you more successful. Whatever your fears are, they are based in lies.

The truth is, you are enough. The truth is, it doesn't matter what others think about you. The truth is, you can do it, whatever "it" may be.

As you identify the lies and choose to believe the truth about yourself, your faith will increase. As your faith gets stronger you will see many more opportunities to create success. While there's always the possibility of failure, remember the message of Distinction 9: Failure is your friend, not your enemy. The fear of failure is one of the primary fears that keep people from taking risks. Successful entrepreneurs understand that failure is just part of the process of success, and fearing it keeps you from moving closer to your dreams and doing what you love. Failure is inevitable. It is foolish to let the fear of something that's inevitable keep you from living your dreams and doing what you love. Success becomes possible when you can go from failure to failure without losing your faith. If you choose faith instead of fear you will eventually achieve true success. If you lose faith after a failure, or failures, you can still choose to have faith again. When it comes to your faith, you can choose it or lose it. Losing faith is simply a choice you make to stop believing. Choosing faith is a choice you make to keep believing that you can and will succeed. Faith says, "Yes you can." Fear says, "No you can't." Whenever your fear tells you that you can't achieve success, just recognize that it is lying to you. Choose to listen to the voice of faith within you.

> Faith says, "Yes you can." Fear says, "No you can't."

Faith is a very real force in the life of many successful entrepreneurs. Faith will motivate you and can give you wise counsel in the hardest of situations. It tells you, "Go for it, you can do it!" It can also say or even shout, *"No! Stop! That is the wrong thing to do!"* Now, there are those confusing times, mostly in the lives of young entrepreneurs, when they took action with faith and still experienced a failure. During those times you might have simply been wrong, or the failure might have been exactly what you needed to experience to give you the knowledge that will empower you to succeed the next time. In a very real way you can actually put your faith in your failures because the belief that failures teach you and are your friend is not some pie-in-the-sky theological theory, it is a very practical reality.

Faith in Numbers

When it comes to the subject of faith and how it relates to business, there is something very practical that you can put your faith in. It is numbers. Some entrepreneurs just put their faith in the mysterious aspects of success and hope for the best. And there is certainly not anything wrong about believing in the mysterious. As one of the most successful entrepreneurs I have ever met has said on numerous occasions, the magic is in the mix. It may sound strange to hear a successful entrepreneur talk about magic. You might think a successful entrepreneur would just look at the bottom-line results, the numbers, not the mysterious. But there is a balance between the practical and the mysterious aspects of business success that many successful entrepreneurs believe in. I can tell you from many personal experiences that there is something powerful about the mysterious side of faith. Just believing, having faith, that you are going to succeed and believing that even if you fail you will learn from it sets you up to succeed no matter what. Part of faith is an expectancy that you will succeed because you already are a success. A personal faith that says "I am successful" will lead to many more successes. Some entrepreneurs who lack faith think *When I experience success then I will be successful,* but truly successful entrepreneurs believe they already are successful.

This mysterious belief that I already am a

successful person empowers entrepreneurs to create practical successes in business. The practical successes in business are revealed in the numbers. One of the most classic examples that reveal a truth about numbers is a batting average in baseball. If someone has a batting average of .300, then that means they hit the ball only three out of ten times at bat. Another way to look at it is they failed to get a hit seven times out of ten. In sales, some salespeople might hear twenty no's, or get twenty rejections for every one yes they get. A young entrepreneur may experience nine failures for every one success. A more seasoned entrepreneur who has already experienced a lot of failures and successes may now be able to experience four successes for every six failures. The most successful stock traders in the world succeed only half the time, which means they lose money on half of all their trades. An inexperienced network marketer might enroll only one out of every ten people they talk to, a more advanced or seasoned network marketer may enroll five out of every ten people.

Once you know the averages in any given industry or profession, you can move forward with faith in the numbers. If you are in sales and you know that the average is twenty no's for every one yes, you can go through the no's, the rejections, with absolute certainty that you are getting closer to a yes. As an entrepreneur, if you know nine out of ten businesses fail, then you can go through the failures knowing you are getting closer to success. So put your faith in the mysterious and the practical.

The mysterious power of faith has two practical names: confidence and perseverance. Confidence comes from the belief, or faith, that I am a successful person and therefore I will succeed. Perseverance is the power to endure and keep on keeping on even when you feel like giving up. Perseverance pays! The combination of confidence and perseverance is a mix of the internal beliefs and external actions. Confidence is the internal belief and perseverance is the external action. Combining the power of confidence and perseverance improves your averages! The more you believe and back up your belief with action, the sooner you'll see the practical, actual, physical, tangible, real world results, called Success.

A Simple Way to Increase Your Faith

I saved the simplest and most powerful way to increase your faith for the end of this book because I want you to remember it and start applying it as soon as you finish reading. It's this: Celebrate your successes. We've all had successes, and if you look, you'll find them throughout your life. Most people don't give themselves enough credit for the things they have been through. Don't let that be you. Think back to times when you were successful and celebrate them. By celebrating times when you were successful in the past, you empower yourself to take risks in the present.

Part of celebrating your successes is being thankful for the challenges that led you to them. We've all had tough times that made us stronger. We've all hit roadblocks that we're now thankful for. Gratitude feeds faith. The more you cultivate gratitude for your life experiences, the more your faith increases. Celebrate by being grateful for your experiences—not just the good ones, but the tough times, too. They're when you probably experienced the most growth.

Every day you can decide to have faith or be afraid. Choose faith. The more often you choose to have faith, the stronger you become and the less power your fears have over you. Keep pressing on. Your faith is your greatest asset. Feed it and find freedom.

Entrepreneurs take risks because of faith.

Employees play it safe because of fear.

Now What?

Visit www.keithcameronsmith.com and sign up for the *Wise Distinctions Newsletter* to continue developing your mind-set for financial and personal freedom. You will also receive updates of live events where you can see me in person.

Share this book with the appropriate people in your life. Discuss the Distinctions with them. Ask them which Distinction is most important for them in their current situations.

Read this book again in a month, and water the seeds you just planted in your mind. I keep my books short and sweet so you can read them again and again.

Invest in the Wisdom Creates Freedom workshop on CD, which includes a full teaching of *The Top 10 Distinctions Between Millionaires and the Middle Class.* In it you'll discover the biggest reasons why some people become financially free and others don't.

ABOUT THE AUTHOR

KEITH CAMERON SMITH is an entrepreneur and inspirational speaker who teaches his life-success principles to individuals and companies across the country. The author of *The Spiritual Millionaire, The Top 10 Distinctions Between Millionaires and the Middle Class,* and other books, Smith lives in Ormond Beach, Florida, with his wife and their two children. Visit www .keithcameronsmith.com.

ABOUT THE TYPE

This book was set in Sabon, a typeface designed by the well-known German typographer Jan Tschichold (1902–74). Sabon's design is based upon the original letter forms of Claude Garamond and was created specifically to be used for three sources: foundry type for hand composition, Linotype, and Monotype. Tschichold named his typeface for the famous Frankfurt typefounder Jacques Sabon, who died in 1580.